THE
TRIAL

How New Labour
purged George Galloway

'When I use a word,' Humpty Dumpty said, in a rather scornful tone, 'it means just what I choose it to mean—neither more nor less.'

'The question is,' said Alice, 'whether you can make words mean so many different things.'

'The question is,' said Humpty Dumpty, 'which is to be master—that's all!'

Acknowledgements

Nicholas De Marco, the young barrister who made such mincemeat of the prosecutors—and for no wages too—and my solicitors Davenport Lyons, especially Kevin Bays, Mark Bateman and Richard Elliot (and their secretaries Jenny Dennis and Claire Wright), all lost this case. But they won the arguments, the credit and my unending gratitude. My witnesses, Tony Benn—the best prime minister Britain never had—Mark Seddon, the bright young editor of *Tribune*, Michael Foot and Tony Woodley, did their best to stop this farce in its tracks (though when I saw the tricoteuse metaphorically knitting through the testimony of such luminaries I knew my head was off). My own staff, Geraldine Clerck, Yasmin Ataullah, Lara Khalidi, James McGowan and David Moxham sustained me through these and many other dark days. So did my wife Dr Amineh Abu-Zayyad and her family who, despite being under military occupation in Palestine, were bombarding me by text with messages of goodwill. My daughter Lucy, Sean Ellis and Jay Stewart, my mother Sheila, sister Colette and brother Graham, my friends Seumas Milne, Brian Dempsey, John Rees, Lindsey German, Teresa Pearce, Rima Husseini, Bob Wylie, John Boothman, John Craig, Mark Craig, Lyn Henderson, Carmel Brown, Andrew Murray, Ma'an Bashour, Nicholas Firzli, Ahmad Kabbara, Ra'if Kasem, Zeid Wehbi, Ron McKay—who also edited this work—Christopher Silvester, Peter Clark, Theresa Gorman, Harold Pinter, Ivan Mulcahey, the Stop the War Coalition for their "Defend George Galloway" campaign, especially Ghada Razuki, Jim Mowatt, Alex Mosson, Christine Hamilton, the Muslim Association of Britain, especially Abu Ubada, Dr Azzam Tammimi, Anas Altikriti, Bill Speirs, Pat Stewart, Betty Brown, Amar Aleman, John Bevan, Andy de la Tour, Wajid Shamsul, Hasan Khawaja Shafique and Salma Yaqoob all made sure than when knocked down, I got up again...and put my feet back on higher ground.

This pamphlet is dedicated to all of them, but above all is dedicated to the people of Palestine and of Iraq, struggling to be free, dignified.
George Galloway MP

Foreword by George Galloway MP

All "show trials" end up demeaning those who prosecute them, and the kangaroo court which expelled me from 36 years membership of the Labour Party was no exception. Damage was done not only to the rights, in a parliamentary democracy, of members of the House of Commons to speak freely on great issues of the day, but to the English language itself. How tortuously the New Labour "prosecutor" squirmed, how inventive the "doublespeak" into which he was forced to lapse. And how uninterested the faceless unknown apparatchiks appointed by the liar, Britain's prime minister Tony Blair, were in the truth, the facts, the consequences of their actions. Theirs was not to reason why…they too were only following orders.

I often sit in parliament looking at the green benches watching a shiver run along looking for a spine to run up. It finds precious few. This "trial" was intended not just to silence me, but to diminish still further the number of spines still standing in what was once a free parliament. "Watch out", New Labour is saying, don't go "too far", or you'll end up on the gallows like Galloway. Only time will tell whether they will succeed in silencing me or intimidating others. Somehow I feel they will succeed in neither. But that is up to you.

If the British people are content to be governed by liars, deceivers, conspirators, those who have joined us by secret diplomacy to the most brutish right wing Republican presidency in the history of the US, then those who people these pages will have triumphed. If on the other hand, those who marched against war, who stand for the rights of working people, who cherish our earth and wish to save it, who oppose racism and religious bigotry, and above all who love liberty can find unity, they can and will be defeated.

The charges

Engaging in conduct which is prejudicial or in an act which is grossly detrimental to the Labour Party, contrary to Rule 2A.8.

1 ...by an interview on Abu Dhabi TV, broadcast to Arab peoples and intended to be heard by an Arab audience, inciting Arabs to fight British troops.

2 ...by an interview on the ITV News Channel inciting British troops to disobey orders.

3 ...inciting Plymouth voters to vote at the next general election against Plymouth South Labour MP Linda Gilroy and Plymouth Devonport Labour MP David Jamieson.

4 ...by an interview on BBC2's *Newsnight* on 22 April 2003 threatening to fight the Glasgow Central constituency in certain circumstances as an independent, ie against a duly endorsed Labour candidate.

5 ...at a public meeting in Preston supporting one Michael Lavalette having stood in local elections in May 2003 against the duly endorsed Labour candidate, Musa Ahmed Jiwa.

The cast of characters

National Constitutional Committee panel chair: Rose Degiorgio-Burley

Barrister for Labour's National Executive Committee (the Presenter): James Goudie QC

Sole witness for the NEC (Presenter): Chris Lennie, deputy general secretary of the Labour Party

Respondent: George Galloway MP

Witnesses for George Galloway: Michael Foot, Tony Benn, Tony Woodley (T&G General Secretary), Mark Seddon (NEC member)

Barrister for the Respondent: Nicholas De Marco

The disciplinary panel met at ISTC, Grays Inn Road, London WC1 on 22 and 23 October 2003

Extracts from the opening argument by Nicholas De Marco

A normal and literal reading of the rules would lead to the inevitable conclusion that the NCC cannot have regard, in relation to a charge under Rule 2A.8, to the interviews and speeches Mr Galloway has given where he expresses his views about the Iraq war. In the circumstances of this case that would mean these charges cannot be brought at all, and the NCC does not thus have jurisdiction to consider them as to do so involves a breach of the rules itself.

Each of the charges against Mr Galloway relate to the expression of his views. There is no other conduct alleged against Mr Galloway. The NEC Presenter claims the charges are nothing to do with expression but about incitement and threats.

If there was any evidence of Mr Galloway committing an unlawful act, such as incitement to treason or throw a brick at a policeman on a demonstration, then such evidence should have been presented by now and the charges appropriately formulated. In those circumstances the National Constitutional Committee could have jurisdiction, we accept, to consider whether such conduct was in breach of Rule 2A.8, subject to the prejudice point discussed later.

But, this is clearly not what the NEC Presenter is pursuing. This is clear from paragraph 7 of Mr Goudie's Summary Response, madam. I think this is a real contradiction in Mr Goudie's whole argument. He says there that intention is not an ingredient to any of the charges. This is paragraph 7 of Mr Goudie's Summary Response. Again intention is not an ingredient of any of the charges.

Therein lies a problem, madam. Incitement or threats require an intention to incite or threaten. Insofar as incitement is to be distinguished from mere expression—this is what the NEC Presenter urges—it must mean more than rousing, which is simply an element of expression, particularly of course of political expression. It must mean incitement to do something which is otherwise in breach of the

Labour Party rules or the general law of the land. The most likely meaning in relation to charges 1 and 2—and what I submit the Presenter really was trying to get at—is incitement to commit the criminal offence of treason or an associated offence, such as disaffection, encouraging disaffection, but this requires an intention to incite a person to commit the offence in question. Any offence of incitement always requires an intention to incite.

It's not, madam, Mr Galloway who formulated the charges, it's not he who says incitement is an ingredient of them. He says, and our case is, that the charges are really just about expression. It's the Presenter who says, "No, they're not about expression, they're about incitement." That is why we make these submissions, because if the Presenter is right and we're wrong on jurisdiction, if they are right that this has nothing to do with expression, it's to do with incitement—and incitement it's to do with—it's incitement to encourage Arabs to fight British troops and encourage British troops to disobey orders—then those two particular charges are extremely serious. They are about the most serious charges that an independent disciplinary panel could decide on. And just think for a moment, madam, those charges, if they were reflected in a criminal court, have the maximum penalty of life imprisonment attached to them. It's as if a disciplinary body was ruling on whether someone had committed murder or not—that's the consequence of it. That's why this submission is extremely serious because of the way my friend seeks to put his charges.

… If the NCC finds Mr Galloway guilty of inciting Arabs to fight British troops, and/or—and that's a word of the charge—and/or of inciting British troops to disobey orders, this clearly prejudices Mr Galloway's right to a fair hearing in relation to the same issues in front of a jury.

The civil proceedings in issue are the defamation proceedings between Mr Galloway and the *Daily Telegraph* newspaper in relation to the latter's allegations that Mr Galloway received money from the previous Iraqi regime. Unfortunately Mr Goudie misunderstands the nature of the issues arising in these proceedings. It is wrong to suggest that the sole issue in the defamation proceedings is a technical defence of qualified privilege. Where the defence of qualified privilege is raised in libel proceedings this does not amount to an admission that the story printed is false—rather the truth of the story is not asserted.

It is important that Mr Galloway should be entitled to argue that a reasonable journalist would not have believed the story at face value. This issue overlaps with the allegations that Mr Galloway supported the Iraqi regime, which is effectively suggested by charges 1 and 2, and certainly charge 1 at least. Further, and more significantly, Mr Galloway's reputation remains a core issue in the defamation proceedings regardless of the *Telegraph*'s choice of defence. Of course the reason why one sues for libel is to protect one's reputation. Reputation remains a central issue throughout the libel proceedings and will be an issue in damages if it goes to that stage. There can be little doubt that the expulsion of Mr Galloway for inciting treason would or could at least have a real risk of prejudicing his reputation.

Chris Lennie cross-examined by Nicholas De Marco

Q: I was going to take you to those minutes in fact next, Mr Lennie, so thank you for that. It's earlier on in the bundle you presented. It's part of—I think it's part of your note in fact. The very last page I seem to recall, page 6, just before you go into detail. If you turn to page 6 please. It's the last paragraph there. It says:
> *"The committee reaffirms that no member shall be disciplined for the mere holding of a belief or opinion, and it will be for the NCC, having seen all the evidence, to determine whether George Galloway has gone beyond the mere holding and the expression of such views."*

Q: I just must confirm again, Mr Lennie, there's nothing in the rules, is there, that says the NCC must determine whether something goes beyond the mere expression of views? That's something you put in. Those words don't exist in the rules, do they?
A: The charges that are laid are to consider whether the conduct of Mr Galloway amounts to prejudicial or grossly detrimental behaviour,

Excerpt from Tony Benn's evidence

Well, at the end of the war, when I came back as a pilot, I heard the preamble of the Charter of the UN. I won't read it because it's here, but it begins, "We the people of the United Nations, determined to save succeeding generations from the scourge of war which twice in our lifetime has brought untold sorrow to mankind..." I am committed to that, I believe that is the only hope for the peace of the world, and I put it here because that also explains the view that those of us took, post the war.

My argument really is that a war is a serious thing, people are killed, and it arouses strong feelings on both sides, and some of the statements that Mr Galloway made were strong.

The prime minister said, "Those who oppose the war had blood on their hands," which is quite a serious charge too, but might indicate to people who are coming to vote at the next election that voting for a candidate who had blood on their hands was quite a serious thing to do, and I think where war occurs you have to expect that not only are strong things done in killing people but strong language is used to put the view of the cardinals, and I did at the end of my statement —and perhaps this is the most important point of all—try and draw attention to the record that the party has on peace.

as per the rules, and that is what the judgment will be.

Q: And do you accept that the formulation of the charges that you say you were responsible for presupposes that this committee must have regard to Mr Galloway's mere expression? Do you accept that?

A: I don't accept that. What they need to do is look at the totality of the behaviours as demonstrated in the charges and the evidence before them as to whether or not in their opinion, in their judgment, that is a set of conducts being demonstrated rather than expressions of—mere expressions of opinion or belief.

Q: And do you accept that the behaviour—evidence of general behaviour of Mr Galloway you rely on under clause—under charge 3, I'm sorry, is to do with mere expression? Do you accept that?

A: I don't accept that either. You know, as was said this morning, what is being demonstrated there is a pattern of behaviour by Mr Galloway, not a mere expression of opinion or belief.

Q: Is it a pattern of expression?

A: It isn't a pattern—it's a pattern of behaviour, not expression.

Q: Behaviour. You're saying it's not expression?

A: It's action, not expression.

Q: Is a speech action or expression?

A: Well, it can be either or both, but can I just—you know what I mean by action. The act of going to a place is an action, the act of encouraging a resultant action by others is an action, expressing a belief is an opinion. That is the distinction. In the charges that are brought it seeks to distinguish from mere expression or holding of opinion to action or the inciting or encouraging of action of others by Mr Galloway.

Q: And if that's a distinction you rely on then you have to accept intent is an ingredient, don't you?

A: I don't have to accept intent. I accept that that is the behaviour that was demonstrated. That is—my investigation was to discover whether there was behaviour that amounted to a case to be heard by the NCC, and that is what I concluded and recommended to the NEC—that there was—and they accepted that judgment and passed the case here.

Q: Well, let's consider inciting Arabs to fight British troops, for instance. You must accept that that requires an intention, doesn't it?

A: I don't accept that it requires an intention. I think it's—it seeks—it seeks to require some sort of outcome.

Q: Isn't that the same thing?

A: I don't think it is.

Q: What's the difference?

A: Well, outcome is something that is encouraged by or had been encouraged on a number of occasions by Mr Galloway on others, which is beyond the mere expression of an opinion.

I mean I'll give you an example. Let me just be clear. For Mr Galloway to say he is for or against something is for him to say he's for or against something. For him to, say, ask others to act upon a belief is a different—of a different order to what his originating opinion might be about something, or his view about something.

Q: So expression's fine as long as you're not trying to convince someone to do something?

A: Freedom of expression is in the rules, as you know.

Q: And it's OK as long as you're trying not to convince somebody to do something?

A: Well, I'd qualify that. I mean the judgment in investigating cases is whether what was—that what had happened, what had occurred, as a result of the actions of Mr Galloway was to bring the party into disrepute. Sorry, was to bring the party—to act in a prejudicial manner to the party or to, you know, grossly disrepute it.

Q: What I'm suggesting to you, Mr Lennie, is in fact you're trying to get round the rules and you're trying to suggest that anything you feel is strongly disagreeable is something you can discipline someone for, despite the fact it's just their view. That's your real intention, isn't it?

A: I don't agree with that, no.

Q: And it must be the case that all politicians—it's a nature of the beast, if you like—try and convince people to do something when they make a speech, don't they?

A: I accept that political behaviour is trying to, you know, persuade change or persuade to a position. That is the nature of political divide. That isn't what we're talking about here.

Q: What about saying the prime minister's a liar?

A: That is a belief that I understand has been expressed.

Q: By a number of Members of Parliament?

A: As I understand it.

Q: Is that mere expression?

A: That is an expression.

Q: Nothing wrong with that?

A: I'm not aware, having investigated any charges that are going to conclude that there is, that those opinions have been expressed.

Q: But I mean you're the one who formulates charges. Do you think that a charge ought to be brought in relation to those sort of allegations?

A: Well, in terms of my role in this, let's just be clear that I was asked to investigate the matter in relation to Mr Galloway, discovered what I discovered, set out what I discovered, and established that in my opinion that it required to be answered, there is a prima facie case to be answered, and that remains my view. There is no investigation that I'm aware of, that I'm involved in, in relation to any other member of the Labour Party having expressed the view of the sort that you've described. But if that's what you're getting at, I'm not aware that that has led to any disciplinary investigation or action.

Q: Do you accept that a lot of constituents of Mr Galloway believed that troops should disobey illegal orders?

A: I do not know the answer to that question because I genuinely have little or no knowledge of the individual constituents of Mr Galloway.

Q: Have you attempted to find out at all what the people of Glasgow Kelvin think?

A: Not as part of this investigation.

Q: Don't you think that's relevant to whether Mr Galloway was expressing unacceptable conduct or was in fact representing, as he has to as a Member of Parliament, commonly held views in his constituency? Don't you think it's relevant?

A: To the investigation into his conduct, no, I don't think it's relevant.

Q: You think it's easy to draw a line between mere expression on the one hand and incitement on the other? Is there a clear line?

A: Well, I don't have a predetermined set of—you know, what's on this side and that side. I don't think it's quite like that, but I in this particular regard have come to the view that we are looking here at behaviour not expressions, conduct not opinions, and it is those that we're asking to be examined and judged by the NCC.

Q: Now, if I could move on to a different area now, Mr Lennie. I just want to ask you whether you're aware yourself, being a deputy general secretary, of any previous NCC decisions where a person's been expelled under Rule 2A.8 in relation to views they expressed. Are you aware of any previous decisions of that nature?

A: I am not personally aware of—I haven't been involved personally in any cases of this sort, so no, I'm not.

Q: Right. That probably answers the next question, but I ought to put it to you anyway—whether you're aware of anyone ever being expelled for incitement?

A: I'm not aware. I haven't been involved in cases of that sort or this sort before, so personally I'm not, which is not the same thing as saying I'm aware of this but I don't have any knowledge.

Q: And incitement's not defined in the Labour Party rules, is it?

A: As far as I'm aware it doesn't appear to be. I probably haven't read them as carefully as you recently, but it doesn't appear to my knowledge.

Q: Now, you're aware of the discussion this morning about disclosure of complaints, and so on. I assume you must have seen a lot of these complaints.

A: Well, not actually, I haven't. I mean what—just so we're absolutely clear about the process that has been undertaken. I was asked by the general secretary, and then subsequently the NEC confirmed, to investigate the conduct, behaviour of Mr Galloway, which is—which is what I did, based upon the letter that Mr Galloway received from the general secretary which is in the bundle before us.

Q: Right, I see, but you're aware of the requests that have been made for disclosure of complaints, I assume?

A: Well, we had that discussion again this morning and, you know, the legal argument—

'Is speech action or expression?' **'Well, it can be either or both'**

Q: It is not the legal, I'm just asking you a question here.

A: Well—

Q: A factual question.

A: You used the term that was in dispute this morning about whether the disclosure or whether a question was asked, and my understanding is that a question was asked and the answer was given. I don't know whether you liked—particularly liked the answer, but that was my understanding of that issue.

Q: I'm happy to use your terminology, Mr Lennie. Are you aware that a question was asked that you ought to disclose all the complaints you'd received about the prime minister's decision to go to war?

A: I'm not aware of—I'm genuinely not aware of the detail of precisely what was asked and what the responses were...

Q: Your solicitors didn't consult you about that request?

A: Pardon?

Q: Your solicitors did not consult you about that request?

A: I was aware that a request was made of that sort and was being dealt with by the—by the solicitors.

Q: Well, we were led to understand that the NEC Presenter took the decision that complaints against the prime minister in relation to the war were irrelevant. Do you now recall making that decision?

A: Irrelevant? Well, the point I think that you made this morning and the point I've just stated was that the case about George Galloway's behaviour does not rely upon complaints having been received from whatever sources about whatever issues. The complaints— the investigation was into the conduct and behaviour of Mr Galloway and it stands on that basis, as per the bundle that we submitted to this hearing.

Q: But you'd accept, wouldn't you, that the NCC should not apply Rule 2A.8 arbitrarily?

A: I—I accept that the NCC is here to exercise its judgment about the case that's presented by the two parties through today and possibly tomorrow. That is their role.

Q: Well, that doesn't really answer the question at all. I mean, I understood that you accept natural justice ought to apply to the proceedings?

A: Yes.

Q: So you do accept that the NCC should not apply this charge arbitrarily?

A: Well, you know, I don't quite understand what you're driving at, but, I mean, I accept that the NCC's role here is to make judgment on the facts as they are discovered through this hearing before them today and tomorrow. That is their role.

Q: Well, you see the question goes to this wording in the rule about prejudice or gross detriment to the Labour Party, Mr Lennie. It's your view, is it, that whether or not conduct is prejudicial to the Labour Party is up to the opinion of the NCC having heard all the evidence?

A: That's the judgment they're asked to make.

Q: And within that bundle of evidence you haven't provided any objective evidence that Mr Galloway's remarks have been prejudicial to the Labour Party, have you?

A: We have—we have set out the evidence of Mr Galloway's behaviours in relation to the five charges and the supporting appendices to that. That's what the case is about.

Q: Yes, and it doesn't include any evidence that the comments were prejudicial to the Labour Party, does it?

A: Well, the charges are predicated on the basis that the conduct is either prejudicial or grossly detrimental to the Labour Party. That is what we're asking the NCC to judge on.

Q: Mr Lennie, I understand your predication of the charges, I'm just saying you haven't submitted any evidence to back that up.

A: That's the judgment that the NCC are asked to reach. That is their role.

Q: Would you accept that there is a wealth of objective evidence to suggest that in fact this whole process is prejudicial to the Labour Party?

A: I'm not aware of it.

Q: What about objective evidence to suggest the prime minister's conduct of the war was prejudicial to the Labour Party? Are you aware of that evidence?

A: I'm not—I'm not aware that that has anything to do with the conduct of Mr Galloway. I mean, you know, here before us is a hearing which is—which is asked to consider Mr Galloway's conduct, not the conduct of the prime minister. I'm aware that there's a whole range of submissions maybe in that bundle which seem to me to be outside of the evidence, but that isn't for me to determine. We've tried to—well, I've tried to stick to the facts as discovered during the investigation.

Q: Yes, I realise why we're here, but it's our case that we ought not to be here, and what I'm saying to you is that you must be aware that the prime minister's support for the war was deeply unpopular with Labour Party members.

Q: Can you tell the tribunal how many members of the Labour Party have resigned as a result of Mr Blair's support for the war?

A: I can't tell you that because I don't know it and I have no information.

Q: You're aware it's a large number, aren't you?

A: As I say, I don't have any information.

Q: Are you aware that there's objective evidence that voters have turned away from the Labour Party as a result of the prime minister's support for the war?

A: Again I'm not aware of your—the kind of causal effect analysis of voter opinion. And I suspect we're going to have a whole series of questions with the same answers.

Q: Well, you are at least aware of the Brent East by-election, aren't you?

A: I'm aware of the result of the Brent East by-election.

Q: And you're aware that that was the first time a sitting Labour parliamentary seat was lost for a very long number of years, aren't you?

A: I am aware of that.

Q: And you're aware that nearly all the commentators, including people in Brent East Labour Party, attribute that to the prime minister's support for the war, aren't you?

A: I'm—you know, I'm aware of a whole lot of things organisationally about the Brent East by-election and lessons the party's learned. That isn't—that isn't actually one of them.

Q: Would you like to turn to Tab 28 of the bundle please, Mr Lennie.

A: 28?

Q: 28, please. There's a series of ICN opinion polls here. Perhaps if you could just turn to the last one, Tab 28, to save going through all of them.

A: Yes.

Q: Question—

A: Tab 28.

Q: Yes, thank you. Question 2: *"Are you satisfied or dissatisfied with the job that Tony Blair is doing as prime minister?"* 61 percent dissatisfied. That's a large number considering the previous popularity of the prime minister, isn't it?

A: Well, it is.

Q: Can you turn to the opinion poll before please, August 2003.

A: One back?

Q: Yes. August 2003 poll. Question 1: *"From what you have seen or heard, do you think the government's report on Iraq's weapons of mass destruction was or was not deliberately embellished to make the case for war?"* Was deliberately embellished 50 percent, was not deliberately embellished 24 percent. Quite a prejudicial opinion poll in terms of the Labour Party's standard really, isn't it?

A: I see the figures.

Q: Question 2: *"Who do you trust more to tell the truth, the BBC, the government, both, or neither?"* The BBC 34 percent, the government 6 percent. Not very flattering.

A: I see the figures, but I'm not quite sure where we're going.

Q: Well, where I'm going is that you're one of the people who for-mulate—you formulated these charges and you were part of the process of bringing this case to the NCC, weren't you?

A: Yes.

Q: Have you ever considered bringing disciplinary charges against the prime minister for conduct which is prejudicial to the Labour Party?

A: I haven't been asked to do so.

Q: Have you considered doing so?

A: Well, I—I haven't been asked to do so. I personally haven't been asked to do so. I don't know if anyone else has been asked to do so, but it's certainly not reached my desk.

Q: You accept, do you, that waging an unlawful and unpopular war is conduct and not mere expression?

A: I don't accept the predications in your statement, as no doubt you'd expect, but again I see no relevance between that and the case we're hearing, to be honest.

Q: Well, Mr Lennie, of course you didn't bring charges against Mr Blair and I'm not sug-gesting you would. You were adult about it, and we're all going to be adult about it. The reason you didn't do that is because you understand, as Labour Party members do, that the prime minister sometimes has to make unpopular decisions and do unpopu-lar things, doesn't he?

A: Well, the prime minister has a hugely res-ponsible job in leading the party and leading the country in government, but that has absolutely nothing to do with why we're here. We're here to consider the conduct of Mr Galloway as set out in the bundle, and I'm not entirely sure where we're going with comparisons as to why the prime minister hasn't been treated in disciplinary hearings of the party.

'How many members... resigned as a result of Mr Blair's support for the war?' 'I can't tell you'

Q: I think any reasonable person could understand the comparison, Mr Lennie. It's this: that there's objective—

A: It's lost on me, I have to say.

Q: It's that there's objective evidence to show the prime minister's conduct has been prejudicial to the Labour Party. It exists.

A: That is your—that is your case. That is what you are submitting.

Q: You have produced no objective evidence that Mr Galloway's remarks are prejudicial to the Labour Party.

A: Well, the evidence submitted was in the case, and I don't intend, as Mr Goudie didn't, to go through that—it has been read by all. Within that it states the case as to why we believe the conducts exhibited by Mr Galloway were either prejudicial or grossly detrimental to the party.

Q: Where is your evidence that it was prejudicial?

A: Well, it's in the bundle. Do you want me to—I'll—

Q: Yes, show me the evidence that it's prejudicial. This is what I've been asking.

A: If I take you from page 3 through to the final Appendix 14.

Q: Page 3 sets out 2A?

A: Yes.

Q: 2A.8.

A: The whole case is contained within it. The charges that we're laying down before the NCC and the evidence of the behaviour of Mr Galloway which we are putting forward as being prejudicial and grossly detrimental to the Labour Party.

Q: Yes, you're arguing that it's prejudicial—you're not putting forward any evidence that it is prejudicial. That's different, isn't it?

A: The whole—the whole of this hearing, the whole of the role of the National Constitutional Committee is to make a judgment about the case. It is my judgment that it was detrimental or prejudicial to the Labour Party—that's why we're here.

Q: Are you really suggesting that there are lots of people who might not vote Labour because of Mr Galloway's remarks?

A: I'm saying that—I'm not making, you know, any grand sweeping statements beyond the evidence that we have before us, and in reaching the conclusion of the investigation, I repeat, that it was my judgment, then shared by Disputes, then shared by Org Committee, then shared by the NEC, that there was a case to be answered about the conduct of Mr Galloway being prejudicial or detrimental to the Labour Party.

Q: The NEC never voted on this, did they?

A: Yes.

Q: The NEC as a whole committee?

A: I can't recall off the top of my head what the sequence of it was, but I think either the Org Committee, which has full delegated powers of the NEC, or the NEC ratified the decision to go for the NCC hearing. I could look at the minutes and check it.

Q: You're aware, aren't you, that the so-called anti-war movement that existed in this country in relation to the Iraq war is the biggest and fastest growing political movement in a generation? You're aware of that fact, are you?

A: I'm aware of the Stop War movement, yes.

Q: Are you aware that the demonstration in February of 2003 was the biggest political demonstration ever to be held in Britain?

A: I'm aware of that.

Q: You're aware of that. And you're aware that Mr Galloway is one of the principal leaders of that movement and was one of the principal speakers at that rally?

A: I'm not sure of any charges that are brought in relation to that.

Q: But you're aware of that, are you?

A: Well, I didn't know George was speaking at it, but it would have surprised me if he hadn't.

Q: Now, surely, considering the unpopularity of the war, having Mr Galloway in the Labour Party is to its benefit rather than its prejudice, isn't it?

A: The issue we're here to look at is whether George Galloway's conduct is prejudicial or grossly detrimental to the Labour Party. If the judgment is that his conduct is prejudicial or grossly detrimental to the Labour Party, then there will be consequences to that. If the judgment is that his conduct has not been prejudicial or grossly detrimental to the Labour Party, then he will remain where he is.

Q: Well, yes, but I thought you were trying to make a case that it was prejudicial, which is why I'm asking you about it. You haven't provided any evidence that it was prejudicial, and I'm suggesting to you that surely it would be for the benefit of the Labour Party to have Mr Galloway within its ranks, wouldn't it?

A: I'll repeat what I said before. The role of investigating and the presentation of the case is to present a case to the NCC in order that they will exercise their judgment about whether his conduct exhibited was prejudicial or grossly detrimental to the party.

Q: It doesn't sound like your heart's really in it then, does it?

A: That's the case that's been brought.

Q: You're not seriously arguing here, are you, that expelling Mr Galloway will help the Labour Party, are you?

'Where are the complaints?' 'I don't have any'

A: No, I'm not calling for any specified predetermined outcome should Mr Galloway be found to have exhibited conduct which is prejudicial or grossly detrimental to the party. That is not my role.

Q: Don't you think that to find Mr Galloway guilty of these charges and to take disciplinary action against him would itself be very prejudicial to the Labour Party?

A: Well, my position is that I believe, having undertaken the investigation, that Mr Galloway has exhibited behaviour which is prejudicial and grossly detrimental to the party, and that is the case we're now discussing. The outcome and the consequences of that are a matter for the NCC.

Q: Let's just turn to the complaints for a minute, Mr Lennie. If you turn to your investigation note, page 3, do you see the second paragraph there? You say:

> "On 24 April the general secretary, David Triesman, wrote to George Galloway MP to advise him that the party were considering whether a formal investigation would be necessary into his conduct."

Yes?

A: Yes.

Q: And you go on to say: "This consideration arose from the receipt of complaints from a number of members of the party."

A: Yes.

Q: You wrote that?

A: Yes.

Q: And it's not true, is it?

A: It is true.

Q: What, that the consideration arose from the receipt of complaints from a number of members of the party?

A: That is what it says, and that is true.

Q: How many members?

A: I don't know how many members. What I'm saying, as I said before, is that the investigation started, was instructed on that basis, and on that basis I acted, but the investigation didn't rely upon, nor does the case rely upon, the complaints of members.

Q: But you just use it here to justify the whole investigation and you now say you don't even know how many members complained.

A: Because what—what gave rise to it [inaudible] part of the investigation. All those things are true.

Q: And earlier in—

A: What I said—sorry to interrupt, but what I said is that the investigation itself did not rely upon, nor does the presentation of this case rely upon, those complaints. The investigation is the behaviour and conduct of Mr Galloway.

Q: ... as part of this evidence of prejudice you rely on. Second paragraph:

> "I confirm that the party has received a number of complaints regarding comments that you have been alleged to have made over the last few weeks. The comments referred to in the complaints concern the role of British troops in Iraq and the possibility of you standing as an independent in Glasgow if you are not selected as a Labour candidate."

That's not true either, is it?

A: That is what it says. Yes, that's true.

Q: What Mr Triesman is saying in that letter is not true, is it?

A: Mr Triesman's—no, what Mr Triesman says in that letter is true.

Q: What, that there were a number of complaints in relation to Mr Galloway standing as an independent in Glasgow? Is that true?

A: Yeah, that's true. That's what it says.

Q: Where are these complaints?

A: I don't have the—I don't have any of this correspondence, but, I mean, that is true. This is what gave rise to the investigation.

Q: Would you accept from me that your solicitors say that bundle A includes the total of communications to the Labour Party calling for action and/or supporting action taken by the Labour Party against Mr Galloway?

A: I take your word for that.

Q: Will you accept from me—and I can give you as long as you like to look for one—that there is not a single complaint within bundle A about Mr Galloway allegedly threatening to stand against a Labour candidate in Glasgow?

A: Yeah. Well, the evidence that points to that is in George Galloway's own mouth, that, you know, as we'll see in the bundle, in an interview given by Mr Galloway I think quite some—I need to go through it in detail to pick it out—he confirms once I think in writing to me that he would consider doing so—I think he used the words in that letter if he was robbed of the opportunity—and in interview he uses similar language, from memory again, that if he was—if Glasgow constituents were cheated of the right to select him, or words to that effect.

Q: Mr Lennie, what I asked you—

A: That's the basis.

Q: What I asked you was whether what was said in Mr Triesman's letter of 21 April 2003 that the has received a number of complaints regarding, amongst other things, the comments Mr Galloway made as to the possibility of him standing as an independent in Glasgow, whether that was true or not. You said it was true.

A: Well, I—

Q: Would you like to reconsider your last answer?

A: I've no reason to doubt it. What I'm saying—what I'm trying to clarify and get clear about is that when I went to investigate these matters it was—it was discovered in a transcript and in a letter then from George Galloway back to me that indeed he had raised the possibility of standing as an independent candidate in certain circumstances, and that is the evidence in the case that we're presenting.

Q: Mr Lennie, you're deliberately refusing to answer the question. You have relied on this letter in your bundle. It's your Appendix 1.

A: Yes.

Q: I am suggesting to you that the Labour Party never received a single complaint, as is suggested in this letter, in relation to standing in Glasgow.

A: Well—

Q: Do you have any evidence to suggest otherwise?

A: I—I believe—it is my view—that the letter that David Triesman wrote to George Galloway is, was and remains true.

Q: Despite the fact that when asked your solicitors have been unable to provide a single letter of complaint, and in correspondence have said they're still trying to get to the bottom of that?

A: You know, I'm—I'm saying that the letter that David Triesman wrote to George Galloway saying that there had been complaints received regarding the comments made about free speech and all that and standing as an—potentially standing as an independent in Glasgow opposite a Labour Party candidate is true.

Q: Mr Lennie, would you accept there is a widely held view in Britain and in the Labour Party that the war against Iraq was illegal?

A: The judgment, as I understand it, provided to government by the Attorney General was that the war was lawful.

Q: And you'd accept, wouldn't you, that there's a widely held view that it was unlawful?

A: Well, I would accept that you get more than one difference of opinion, sure, but in terms of what action was taken—but I don't actually see the relevance of the position in relation to different views around about the legality of the war.

Q: Well, you'll see the relevance when we move on to charge 2—it's directly relevant. Would you accept that 139 Labour MPs voted against a war?

A: From memory I can't recall, but certainly people voted against going to war.

Q: And that was the biggest rebellion suffered by a governing party in British history?

A: Again I don't know the detail, but I see what you're saying.

Q: So we're talking about a very controversial issue with strong feelings roused. You'd accept that?

A: Absolutely.

Q: And you heard Mr Benn's evidence this morning that a lot of people did feel very strongly about it, and that was reflected in their language?

A: Yes. I'd expect nothing less at the time of war.

Q: Would you accept that numerous eminent lawyers and the vast majority of international lawyers believed that the war was unlawful?

A: I have honestly no idea about that question.

Q: You can turn to Tab 10 if you like, if you want to have a look. You may not have your appendices to Mr Galloway's—if you turn past these World Socialist Web Site pages to something from the *Guardian*. It's the last of the extracts. Sorry, not the last, it's the penultimate extract in Tab 10. It's an article on Friday 14 March 2003. *"Law unto themselves"*. Sorry.

The chair: Which page?

Mr De Marco: *"Law unto themselves. A large majority of international lawyers reject the government's claim that UN Resolution 1441 gives legal authority for an attack on Iraq."*

And I'll just take you to the first paragraph.

"Military action against Iraq under existing UN resolutions would be unlawful, despite claims to the contrary by ministers. This is the near-unanimous view of international lawyers on an issue which has profound implications for future relations between sovereign states."

A: I can read it.

Q: And if you could turn to Tab 5 for a moment please, this is an extract from the *Independent* newspaper on 19 March 2003 which deals with the backbench rebellion we mentioned earlier, and I think you'll see over the page the government motion. This was the motion that supported the war. And do you see that says:

> "Iraq's weapons of mass destruction and long-range missiles pose a threat to international peace. Iraq has not cooperated actively, unconditionally and immediately with the weapons inspectors and has rejected the final opportunity to comply. The UK seeks a new UN Security Council resolution on the rebuilding of Iraq and welcomes the imminent publication of a road map towards a just and lasting peace settlement for Israel."

Do you accept that the war on Iraq as reflected in the first sentence there was predicated—the legality of it was predicated on the basis that Iraq had weapons of mass destruction?

A: You know, you're asking me a whole range of questions which I'm not going to be terribly helpful with. All I—I can read the motion that it says there, I can read the voting figures it says there, I can read the reports there, and I confirm that that's what they say. Do you want my opinion about something or…

Q: Just that—

A: …or on the facts?

Q: Just that you would accept on reading that motion that the war was predicated on the belief that Iraq had weapons of mass destruction?

A: I think there were a whole range of reasons and implications and factors involved.

Q: And you referred earlier I think to the Attorney General's opinion. Do you accept that he also based his support for the legality of the war on the basis that Iraq possessed weapons of mass destruction?

A: All I'm saying is that my understanding is, humble as it is, that the advice that was given was that the action against Iraq was lawful. That's—I don't know what it's based on, I haven't researched it, and so I'm probably not very helpful in terms of the legal detail.

Q: Would you like to turn to Tab 16 of the bundle. This is the infamous September dossier, and I only want to take you to the foreword by the prime minister, if I may. This was the foreword he put in this dossier when it was laid before Members of Parliament.

Could you go to the third paragraph. Do you see at page 3 where it starts, the foreword?

A: Beginning "In recent months…"

Q: Yes, the last part of the sentence where it says:

> "Saddam Hussein is continuing to develop weapons of mass destruction and with them the ability to inflict real damage upon the

region and the stability of the world."

That was what Mr Blair was telling parliament, wasn't it?

A: That's what the dossier says.

Q: Go down to the fifth paragraph.

"What I believe the assessed intelligence has established beyond doubt is that Saddam has continued to produce chemical and biological weapons, that he continues in his efforts to develop nuclear weapons, and that he has been able to extend the range of his ballistic missile programme."

A: Yes.

Q: Yes?

A: Yes, I read it.

Q: Two more paragraphs down.

"I am in no doubt that the threat is serious and current, that he has made progress on weapons of mass destruction and that he has to be stopped."

Yes?

A: Yes.

Q: And finally over the page—penultimately over the page, the first paragraph on that page.

"And a document discloses that his military planning allows for some of the weapons of mass destruction to be ready within 45 minutes of an order to use them."

You'll be familiar with that claim, no doubt?

A: [Witness nodded in the affirmative]

Q: And two more paragraphs down.

"The threat posed to international peace and security when weapons of mass destruction are in the hands of a brutal and aggressive regime like Saddam's is real."

Yes?

A: Yeah, that's what it says.

Q: So Tony Blair certainly was selling the war on the basis of Iraq's possession of weapons of mass destruction?

A: That's what the dossier foreword says, and I can confirm to you that you've read that.

Q: And that has now been demonstrated to be misconceived or untrue, hasn't it?

A: Well, there's a whole lot of things that have happened since then, but that was

'You're aware it's not a complete transcript?' 'I accept that'

the position at that time.

Q: In fact, Mr Lennie, even at the time of the September dossier revelations there were those around the prime minister who were aware that there was no imminent threat from Iraq, weren't there? Are you aware of that?

A: I'm sure there was a discussion about whether we go to war [inaudible].

Q: If you'd like to turn to Tab 15 of the bundle, please, you'll see this is the e-mail from—e-mail produced in full from the prime minister's chief of staff, Jonathan Powell, to the chairman of the Joint Intelligence Committee—this had to be disclosed in relation to the Hutton Inquiry—an e-mail sent on 17 September.

If you go to the third paragraph.

"First, the document..."—that's the September dossier—"...does nothing to demonstrate a threat, let alone an imminent threat, from Saddam."

Yes?

A: The document—yes, that's what it says, yes.

Q: Mr Lennie, if you could turn to Tab 19 please.

A: 19?

Q: Yes, please.

A: I might not know anything about this either.

Q: It's an observation made in Mr Robin Cook the former foreign secretary's book. It's referred to in the first paragraph that Tony Blair privately conceded two weeks before the Iraq war that Saddam Hussein did not have any usable weapons of mass destruction.

You're aware Mr Cook's made that claim?

A: Well, I'm reading these, but I haven't read Robin Cook's book, but I can read what the words say there, and I can confirm that you're reading it as set down there.

Q: Do you agree that that's tantamount to saying that the prime minister deceived parliament?

A: I'm saying I'm agreeing that you read out what you read out and that is what it says. I have no knowledge of it.

Q: Yes. Do you agree that what Mr Cook is saying is tantamount to saying the prime minister deceived parliament?

A: I repeat again—and we're not going to get very far, but I haven't had that discussion, I haven't heard Robin Cook say that, I haven't read his book, etc. I'm aware he resigned from the cabinet.

Q: I shan't ask you any more directly about the legality of the war,

Mr Lennie.

A: OK.

Q: But I will start addressing the various charges that you have formulated, starting with your charge 1 please.

Now, if we could first look at your Appendix 7. This is the transcript that you relied on to formulate charge 1, isn't it?

A: Yes.

Q: There's no other evidence you relied upon?

A: No, this is it.

Q: This is it?

A: That's it.

Q: And you accept this is an incomplete transcript?

A: I accept that this is a transcript provided for us through the BBC. I had discussions with George about this transcript I think on 18 June and George raised concern that it may not be fully accurate in every detail and exactly a verbatim account of what he said, but we got to the position—and I'm summarising—that it was agreed between us that in terms of the investigation it could be relied upon as being a reasonable and fair reflection of what George said during the interview.

Q: You're aware that it's not a complete transcript?

A: I've said what I said, and I know that—the word "complete"—if you mean that it isn't a verbatim account of that interview, you know, I accept that.

Q: You accept that?

A: Because I don't—I don't have Abu Dhabi TV, I wasn't there. I did discuss it with George in our—in our interview, or in our discussions on 18 June.

Q: Do you accept that there's lots of this transcript where the person transcribing writes "indistinct" because they don't know what was actually said?

A: Yes. That's what it says.

Q: And you accept that the way in which this transcript was made was that somebody translated Mr Galloway's words into Arabic and then some other person, anonymous person, translated the Arabic again back into English and wrote down this?

A: That appears to be the case. When I discussed it with George I'm aware that—you know, he obviously was conducting his interview in English, but I understand that it was broadcast to—via Abu Dhabi TV, that it was dubbed over in Arabic.

Q: In Arabic?

A: And I think it's probably reasonable to conclude that it was then

Charge One

translated back and this is what we've got. I'm not actually certain of that, but I think that's reasonable, I accept that.

Q: So the translation—this translation was a translation of an Arabic translator?

A: I don't know. I don't know.

Q: What I mean—I should put that slightly differently. There's such a chain here.

A: That is—from English to Arabic and—

Q: This translation is not a translation of what Mr Galloway says, but it's a translation of what an Arabic person said Mr Galloway said?

A: I think that—that seems to be the case.

Q: That's pretty unreliable evidence in terms of something where one is facing a charge on exact words used, isn't it?

A: Well, I accept—I accept there are sort of complications around it, but, you know, it is my evidence that I discussed this with George. This was presented to him in a note prior to my meeting with him on 18 June, and, you know, I'm not quoting verbatim, I'm not trying to put words in Mr Galloway's mouth, but in terms of facilitating and processing the investigation it was agreed between us that it could be—it reflected, you know, in reasonable—reasonable sense what he said during that interview, and obviously the particular paragraphs that are concerned come right at the end of that interview. Those are the ones that are highlighted and those are the ones that, you know, are the subject of this hearing. But it's here in its entirety.

Q: And do you accept that Mr Galloway has always denied he was inciting Arabs to fight British troops?

A: Well, I don't want to sort of speak for Mr Galloway, other than what I know in terms of my meeting with him, and, you know, on the basis of our discussion we've included this to form part of the evidence at this NCC hearing.

Q: Now, Mr Lennie, despite the fact that this is, as you accept, an inaccurate and unreliable transcript, you weren't satisfied with it and you adopted it even further, didn't you?

A: Well, I'm not sure I adopted it. Can I just be clear. At Appendix 8 of the bundle, which is the interview that was on the ITV News Channel on 1 April, there's a question asked then to George by the presenter about this issue. It appears on page 32. The presenter says to George, *"But you yourself are almost inciting more trouble in the Middle East, aren't you?"*, and it goes on with questions and you can read it, and George's answer is, *"Well, I don't think they need much incitement from me."*

Q: So what?

A: Well, you know, it stands for itself.

Q: It stands for what? What do you say that says?

A: Well, if—if what you said before, that George Galloway was keen to deny any attempt to incite, I would have thought that would have been the point at which he would deny that that was what he had done.

Q: Well, he's saying he doesn't need to deny it.

A: When asked the direct question.

Q: He's saying there he doesn't need to deny it.

A: That's your interpretation.

Q: He's said elsewhere, hasn't he, that he did deny it?

A: I don't know that, but I'm—I'm relying on the evidence we've presented here.

Q: Well, I'll come back to that in a moment.

A: It seems to me to support the view that the presenter's interpretation was that this was almost an incitement, and George's response was that the Arab leaders wouldn't need much incitement from him.

Q: I suggest that actually goes nowhere at all to help your case, Mr Lennie. If you turn to page 8, this is your version, what you thought—

A: Page 8?

Q: Page 8 of your...

A: Bundle.

Q: ...bundle.

A: Yes.

Q: This is the way you seek to present the case to this tribunal.

A: Yes.

Q: And you accept there that you have taken those parts of the transcript—the inaccurate transcript—that you think Mr—that you think prejudice Mr Galloway, and you relied on them ignoring all the other parts of the transcript. You've taken them out of context, haven't you?

A: I believe that those are the parts of the transcript which highlight the offence as laid out in the charges.

Q: And you've ignored the missing words?

A: I haven't ignored them, they're there in the whole bundle of evidence, but in terms of focusing on what the offence—where the offence occurs I've taken those from the transcript and put them in the charge as laid.

Q: You deliberately do not include the remarks that the transcript says Mr Galloway says where he's attributed as saying, *"It's not practical*

Exctract from Michael Foot's supporting statement

I am disturbed, as I think many people in the Labour Party will be, by the apparent willingness of the NEC Committee and the NEC itself to reach a decision on George Galloway's case before the conclusion of the dispute between Galloway and the Daily Telegraph. *The* Daily Telegraph *has made a series of defamatory statements against him which he is seeking to defeat by the proper legal process.*

A premature decision by the NEC Committee on other aspects of the case might injure his position. So I hope in common fairness the NEC will be ready to postpone the judgement until the Daily Telegraph *case is concluded.*

I have been a strong opponent of the war, as have millions of others in our country, in the United Nations and within our party. I fundamentally disagree with the Labour Party's part in it. I have called for the prime minister to review his position, believing that he misled the country and parliament. I have seen George Galloway's legal argument and agree with it. It is my view that the war was illegal, unjust and immoral.

for other armies to support Iraq." You miss those out, don't you?

A: I've not deliberately—well, I have—I have chosen what I believe to be and I have highlighted, established, set out briefly the remarks that demonstrate conduct which is prejudicial or grossly detrimental to the Labour Party.

Q: But how can you do that if in one sentence it says, *"Why don't Arabs do something for the Iraqis? Where are the Arab armies?"* You try and give that a certain meaning, and then in the next sentence it makes quite clear that Mr Galloway's not calling on any armies to intervene. That's not a fair presentation of the case, is it?

A: That is my presentation of the case, that that statement was intended to be broadcast on Arab TV to Arab peoples, and the intention for the purpose of that quote was aimed at Arab peoples.

Q: The intention was that the interview was aimed at Arab peoples. That's as far as you go, is it, with the intention?

A: This was aimed at Arab peoples—to incite, as we say in the charges, Arab peoples to rise in support of the Iraqis against coalition forces. That's my interpretation.

Q: And you get to that by taking out those parts of the interview that don't help that interpretation that you seek to put, don't you?

A: I get to that by the quotes that I've put in the charge sheet.

Q: Selective, out of context quotes.

A: I get to that by the quotes and I stand by those quotes.

Q: Now, can I just ask you how this so-called transcript came to your attention in the first place?

A: It came to—it came to us through the BBC's Media Monitoring, or the BBC I suppose World Service Monitoring.

Q: It's not how it first came to your attention, is it?

A: Well, I don't know how it first came to anyone's attention, but that's how we got the transcript.

Q: How did all of this get into the public domain?

A: I'm not quite sure what you're getting at. The transcript is what I've relied upon in terms of the investigation.

Q: Yes, and you're saying that Mr Galloway's interview was prejudicial to the Labour Party. How did the interview get into the public domain?

A: I don't quite follow you. I mean I suppose it was reported. Is that what you're suggesting?

Q: Well, you don't know, you haven't looked into this at all as part of your investigation.

A: It hasn't formed part of my bundle of evidence. The bundle of evidence is here and we have here the broadcasts. What we're saying about this is that Mr Galloway chose to do an interview on Abu Dhabi TV to an Arabic audience, in English these things were said, and in my view that is—that is the basis of this charge. They were intended to incite a reaction amongst Arab peoples in support of Iraq against British troops.

Q: Let me just slow you down a moment. How do you say the interview prejudices the Labour Party?

A: I'm saying that this interview and plainly the remarks are inciting Arab peoples to rise up against British troops at a time of war. That is what we're putting forward as being conduct prejudicial and grossly detrimental to the Labour Party.

Q: Mr Galloway never talks about British troops or rising up against British troops or fighting British troops, does he?

A: The interview is there, the quotes are there. I refer to my evidence on them.

Q: Now, it's the case, isn't it, that this story came into the public domain via Mr Adam Ingram MP, the armed forces minister, didn't it?

A: I honestly do not know whether that's true or not. I have no evidence to offer on that.

Q: Well, you'll see—and I assume you've read the witness statements in this case—that it's Mr Galloway's case, and Mr Seddon [Mark, NEC member] supports his case with evidence, that Mr Ingram deliberately put this story in the public domain as an attempt to prejudice Mr Galloway.

A: That is not my evidence, so I don't know about that.

Q: This story would have gone unnoticed, but the transcript provided to Mr Ingram through his connections as an armed forces minister with this reporting centre led Mr Ingram to feed this story to the *Sun* newspaper. You're aware of that?

A: I'm just curious about your statement that this report—this interview would have gone unnoticed.

Q: Well, it was broadcast in Abu Dhabi. There's not many Labour voters in Abu Dhabi.

A: I imagine that people do watch Abu Dhabi TV. I don't, but I imagine that it is received…

Q: Have you investigated that?

A: …in Arab nations and possibly even others.

Q: Have you investigated that?

A: I assume that's the purpose.

Q: Have you investigated that?

A: I haven't investigated it, but I'm making an assumption.

Q: An assumption. This interview got into the public domain in Britain through Mr Ingram encouraging the *Sun* to report this story.

A: I—I don't know if that's true or not and I'm not sure there's evidence.

Q: Mr Ingram did that in order to blacken Mr Galloway's name at the time Mr Galloway was a leader of the anti-war movement.

Mr De Marco: Perhaps we could consider charge 2.

The chair: Yes.

Mr De Marco: Now, Mr Lennie, I'll suggest that once again you have quoted selectively from a transcript that you were provided of what Mr Galloway was supposed to have said in an interview, haven't you?

A: Yeah, I've taken what I believe to be the—what you might call offensive conduct from that interview and highlighted it in the charge. The quote, *"So three British soldiers…"* etc.

Q: Yes. And the way you put it in your note is, *"So three…"*—this is page 8, madam.

> *"So three British soldiers are already on their way back to England to face court martial for refusing to obey illegal orders and the others should do so too. The three of them were right to do so."*

They are the parts of the interview you select, aren't they?

A: They are.

Q: And let's just look at what the transcript says Mr Galloway actually said, and this is at Tab 8 of the bundle, madam… And in answer to a question about, you know, *"What do you mean disobeying or ignoring illegal orders?"* Mr Galloway says:

"You sound surprised. The government's own principal legal adviser in the Foreign Office resigned from her job for precisely that reason, and Kofi Annan, the secretary general of the United Nations, who are in charge of international law, has stated that this is an illegal war. So there isn't much controversy about it being an illegal war, and the idea of obeying illegal orders died at the war crimes tribunal in Nuremberg at the end of the Second World War. So three British soldiers are already on their way back to England to face court martial for refusing to obey illegal orders and the others should do so too."

Now, Mr Lennie, putting it in that context, doesn't that give an entirely different view of what Mr Galloway said than this selective quoting you rely on?

A: What I've highlighted are the parts of quotations from George Galloway's interviews that caused the charge to be made. The bundle, quite rightly, contains the documents to give it context there, it's been read by all, and the panel will make its judgment about it.

Q: In fact what you were doing is you were straining to create an inventor charge by omitting the context in which Mr Galloway's remarks were made, weren't you?

A: I've not tried to omit anything. The whole Appendix 8 bundle is there in its entirety. What I've tried to do is take from that the remarks made which are aimed at inciting British soldiers to disobey their orders.

Q: Disobey illegal orders—yes?

A: Well, the quote is *"illegal orders"*.

Q: Yes. So the charge—let's have a look at the charge for a moment. Charge 2. The charge—particulars: *"Inciting British troops to disobey orders."* This is page 1, madam.

The chair: Yes.

Mr De Marco: That's actually wrong, isn't it?

A: Not in my judgment.

Q: Mr Galloway was not inciting people to disobey orders. You say yourself his comments are only in relation to illegal orders, aren't they?

A: Well, you know, the charge sheet is there that—it is put before the panel that George's conduct was intended to get British soldiers to disobey their orders. The quote—the quote that I've put is there and the transcription is in full for the panel to see. It is put before the panel that George's remarks were made intended—with a view that it was to influence British soldiers in refusing to obey their orders. That is—that is the charge 2 that I've brought.

Q: Just before I go into that, you used the word "intended" there. Was that a mistake by you?

A: Well, probably. I mean the purpose of George's—George Galloway's remarks were to produce an action, and that action was that—that action was for British soldiers to refuse to obey their orders.

Q: Do you think your charge would sound a bit different if you said that Mr Galloway was trying to encourage British troops to disobey illegal orders? Do you think that would sound different?

A: I don't think it's relevant.

Q: Do you think it would sound different?

A: It would be a different word, but it wouldn't be relevant to the charge that we put.

Q: It would be irrelevant to the charge you put, but it would be relevant to the facts because Mr Galloway never suggested people disobey orders, he suggested that people only disobey illegal orders, didn't he?

A: The circumstances at the time of his interview were that British troops/coalition forces were at war in Iraq, and George Galloway, Labour MP, gave his interview, during which he made these comments about what British soldiers should do.

Q: Do you think that British soldiers should obey illegal orders?

A: I think British soldiers should obey their orders.

Q: Even if they're illegal?

A: They should obey their orders.

Q: Even if they are illegal?

A: Well, the issue here is not about illegal or legal orders, the issue here is about George's conduct in seeking to get British soldiers not to do what they're told by their superiors.

Q: Now, Mr Lennie, perhaps you could answer the question. Do you think British troops should obey illegal orders?

A: Well, I think the issue here is George's well-known view, he expressed it, he's expressed it before that the war was illegal, etc, etc. The fact of the matter is that we were at war in Iraq at this time, British troops were there fighting under orders, and the intention—sorry, I won't use that word—the purpose of these remarks was to get British soldiers to disobey the orders they were given during that war.

Q: Illegal orders. Let's just stop changing the words. It's illegal orders only, isn't it?

A: That's Mr Galloway's view.

Q: Now, what would happen if—and it's been widely reported—a particular officer in the army instructed his soldiers to shoot at unarmed Iraqi civilians? Do you think they should obey that order?

A: You're dealing with hypotheticals, I'm dealing with circumstances that applied at the time that British troops were at war under orders in the pursuit of that war, and George called on them to disobey those orders.

Q: I have to put it to you, Mr Lennie, that your position is the position that the war criminals of the Hitler regime argued in their defence in Nuremberg, isn't it?

A: My position is the one I've just stated to you. British troops were at war in Iraq, George Galloway gave his interview on ITV News, ITN News, when he called for British troops to disobey the orders in line with the three who he quotes had also done so.

Q: German troops were at war in 1939 to 1945, weren't they? They were at war—yes?

A: Mmm.

Q: They were given orders, and their defence to war crimes was that they obeyed them because they had to obey orders. That's not a legitimate argument any more, is it?

A: The context—we've gone through the government's position in relation to the war, the coalition forces' position in relation to the war we've been through before. The circumstances of this interview, British troops were at war in Iraq fighting with coalition forces against Saddam and his regime, and Mr Galloway called on the British soldiers to refuse to obey their orders.

Q: Now perhaps if Mr Galloway had called on British soldiers to refuse to obey their orders you might have a point, if he said British soldiers should refuse to obey any orders given to them you may have a point, but nowhere does Mr Galloway make that suggestion, does he?

Q: Yes, this is an extract from the *Times* newspaper…

A: Yes.

Q: …of 30 March 2003, and it's about the three soldiers that Mr Galloway is talking about in his interview. Look at the—in fact the

'British soldiers should obey their orders'
'Even if they're illegal?'
'They should obey their orders'

first sentence is:

> "*Two soldiers sent back from the Gulf after expressing concerns about the legality of the Iraq war will not face disciplinary action, their lawyer said yesterday.*"

And then if you go to not the next paragraph but the one after:

> "*The soldiers, whose names have not been made public, were said to have been inspired by the resignation from the cabinet of Robin Cook, the former foreign secretary, to question whether the conflict was justified. Their solicitor suggested the government was reluctant to allow the legality of the Iraq war to be put on trial by punishing the men.*"

Have you taken any disciplinary action against Robin Cook for inciting British soldiers to disobey illegal orders?

A: I've not been asked to investigate Robin Cook's conduct.

Q: Do you think you ought to, having read this?

A: I don't believe there is a case to investigate, as far as I'm aware, in terms of Robin Cook.

Q: You notice that the soldiers who disobeyed illegal orders do not claim to have been inspired by Mr Galloway, or even mentioned him—they claimed to be inspired by Mr Cook?

A: Mr Galloway's interview was given after—after these soldiers had, as I understand it, refused to obey their orders.

Q: Go down to five more paragraphs I think that starts "*Mr Blade…*"

> "*Mr Blade said the Robin Cook resignation was the sort of focal point. That really sparked it up and fanned it up. They're getting bombarded with propaganda that this was an illegal war or it would be an illegal war if it went without United Nations support. They are doubtful about whether it was a legal war.*"

Quite clear from the soldiers' point of view, that is, that it's a question of illegal orders that they object to, isn't it?

A: All I can say is that the words you've read are correct, and I'm not quite sure—you know, I haven't given it any thought in terms of interpreting it, nor do I think it's relevant to the case—to this case.

Q: Can you go down a couple more paragraphs please:

> "*Mr Blade said that the men were sent home to prevent their views spreading and taking root. They have now been told that no disciplinary action will be taken and nothing will go on their records. 'I believe that the Ministry of Defence were reluctant to initiate any legal proceedings because they know that our case will be that it was an illegal war,' he said.*"

That's the solicitor. Now, isn't it rather strange to charge someone with inciting something which the thing they are supposed to have incited doesn't even get them a court martial in the army?

A: The charge here is that George Galloway gave an interview during which he called upon British soldiers to disobey their orders—described by him, as you say, as illegal orders. That is the charge. My understanding is that there isn't any difference between us that that is what happened. George—the interview, the transcript, is accurate, the extracts from it are accurate, and the charge stands on its own facts.

Q: Let's move on to charge 3. So, so far Mr Galloway is saying to you it's not an accurate representation, isn't he?

A: Well, he's saying that—you know, his statement is that it couldn't bear the meaning that I believe it contained. That is what he's saying.

Q: And before that, in answer to your question about the accuracy, he is pointing out a number of problems with the accuracy, isn't he?

A: Yes, he's pointing out that it isn't verbatim—I accept it's not verbatim—and there's been a triple translation—I accept there's been a triple translation. The point I—the evidence I gave before and I'll repeat here is that broadly speaking, "The word is the words that you spoke during that interview," and I think we're agreed that broadly speaking, you know, to the point where the substance of what was said between us I think is confirmed in this discussion. I am reading as we go along.

Q: Yes. Well, I'm looking to find that confirmation. Let's look at your next question, which starts at a paragraph what, halfway down that.

"...however, it has been established by whoever it has been established, someone in the BBC monitoring service, is reliable as a set of factual statements of what you actually said."

And in answer to that point Mr Galloway says:

"I know, I accept it is a foreign person speaking English and therefore it's not obviously exactly in my words, it's a kind of pidgin English..."

And the next sentence:

"But it's my point that the material or salient passages in the transcripts are not capable of bearing the meaning..."

Again two points. He's saying it's not his words, and anyway it's not capable of bearing the meaning you attribute to it. That's the two points he makes there, isn't it?

A: I—I took that to mean that we were agreed that there was material and salient passages. We knew what they were, we discussed them. The material and salient passages are there. There is—clearly there's

'It's not pretty accurate, I accept that'

a difference here, there's a difference there, in terms of whether they're capable of bearing the meaning that the charge puts on them, but that isn't the same thing as saying that they weren't said.

Q: And finally on this point, over the page, he again repeats the second point. The first paragraph over the page:

"…I am saying that that transcript, even with the caveats, is not capable of bearing the two meanings that you ascribe to me."

So I suggest to you that there's three things you can draw from this interview, Mr Lennie, and no more. The first is that Mr Galloway denies it's an accurate transcript of what he said—yes?

A: Well, what George says is that it is subject to the caveats and omissions from the translation, and it is his position that it can't bear the meaning that the has put on it, and, you know, the confirmation of that on page—I think it's page 3, it's not numbered, but under the paragraph that you've read out, and I said back to George *"I hear that. That general thought. But that will be an argument if there is a case brought at a future time at the NCC."*

Q: We're not interested in what you say.

A: Well, that is—that is what was said at that time and George's reply was *"Sure."*

Q: Yes, but what does that show? That of course this will be subject to an argument here. I'm putting to you, and perhaps you could answer the question, that there's three things that this interview shows and you've just gone on to the second. The first is Mr Galloway says throughout that it was not an accurate transcript of the interview.

A: It's not pretty accurate, I accept that. *"It's not a verbatim account"* is what he says.

Q: The second point is that he says he only accepts it subject to the caveats in his letter—yes?

A: That is his position, yes.

Q: And the third point he makes is that even with those caveats and even though it's not accurate he doesn't believe you can attribute the meaning to it.

A: That's his position.

Q: That's his position. Not that he was in some way satisfied, as you tried to suggest to the panel earlier, with this transcript as being an accurate record. That is never how Mr Galloway has presented the case.

A: Yeah. What I said to the panel, and I'll say it again, is that it served the purpose of establishing pretty close to fully accurately what George said, and what the difference between us is the meaning that those words can bear, and that is what I said at the time would become an argument should there be a case—I hadn't decided whether a case would be brought or not at that time—at the NCC, and, you know, that has turned out to be the case.

Q: Yes. And you think it's appropriate to bring what is effectively a charge of treason on this sort of inaccurate transcript, do you, with no other evidence? You think that's appropriate?

A: Well, what the charge is is that during an interview on Abu Dhabi TV broadcast to Arab peoples, intended to be heard by an Arabic audience, he incited Arabs to fight British troops. That's what— that is the charge.

Q: Yes. Now, you said before that Mr Galloway never denied that he incited British—Arabs to fight British troops.

A: Well, in the interview—what I said before is in the interview he was offered the opportunity—I think the ITV News interview from memory—he had the opportunity to deny and didn't.

Q: But elsewhere he did deny, didn't he?

A: That isn't part of the bundle of evidence.

Q: Isn't it? Are you sure about that?

A: Well, that—

Q: Have you read your own evidence?

A: That is—that is the evidence I presented, but let me just get the quote again.

Q: We know the quote you're relying on, but you've just said that it's not in the bundle of evidence that Mr Galloway denies the charge. I'm asking you, are you sure about that?

A: I'm standing by when given the opportunity by the presenter in the interview at Appendix 8, when asked the question, *"You your-self are almost inciting more trouble, aren't you? Because on the inter-view you said, 'When are the Arab leaders going to wake up?'"* etc, his reply was, *"Well, I don't think they need much incitement from me."* That is my evidence.

Q: It doesn't really go to anything, that. Would you like to turn to your Appendix 2. Now, this is a letter I think before you were even involved with the operation, but it's your appendix. It's a letter to Mr Triesman, the general secretary, from Mr Galloway, and there's a postmark at the top, 29 April 2003. So it's shortly after this issue came to light. And if you go halfway down that letter Mr Galloway says:

"Let's go to the heart of the issue. I did not call the British armed forces wolves, indeed I called them lions. I did not call upon the British armed forces to disobey orders, I called upon them to disobey illegal orders. As you well know, this is in fact a legal obligation on them, as on all armies and all governments since Nuremberg. I did not call upon anyone to kill British soldiers, I said the British forces should be withdrawn before more were killed in this action."

Do you now accept that as far back as April of this year Mr Galloway did clarify that he never called—he never incited anybody to shoot or kill British troops?

A: What the charge says George did on the one hand was give an interview on Abu Dhabi TV, the one that is the subject of the discussion we had previously about accuracy, non-accuracy and completeness, and the charge is that that was broadcast on Arab TV to Arab peoples, intended to be heard by an Arab audience, inciting Arabs to fight British troops.

Q: And would you like to—

A: That's—that's the charge that is laid. Secondly, the charge is laid that he also in an interview on ITN News—ITV News, ITN News, gave an interview in which he incited British troops to disobey audience—disobey their orders.

Q: Yes. Mr Lennie, you have presented in evidence today, and Mr Goudie has said in his summary response, one of the main points you make against Mr Galloway is that he never denied he incited British troops to—sorry, incited Arabs to attack British troops. Do you accept that this letter of 29 April constitutes such a denial? That's all the question is, Mr Lennie. Please answer that question.

A: Well, can I just say what I did say. What I said is that in an interview the ITN News presenter offered him the opportunity by asking the question about whether he was inciting more trouble in the Middle East, he didn't take that opportunity to deny that, rather the quote was, *"Well, I don't think they need much incitement from me."* That is the evidence. And that interview was given, as you know, on 12 April 2003.

Q: Mr Lennie, just before I take you further, don't you accept this is all a mockery? There's absolutely no statement by Mr Galloway in a triple translated inaccurate document that he's calling for Arabs to fight British troops. He confirms in April that that certainly was not what he was doing, he's maintained that position throughout, and you're trying to bring a charge effectively of treason on the basis of your impression of extracts from a translated transcript. It's mockery, isn't it, Mr Lennie?

A: Well, I think it's very serious indeed, and I think that's why we're here, and quotes that we've used are quotes we've taken from the interview that George gave to Abu Dhabi TV and subsequently given the opportunity on 1 April on ITV News to deny that that was his purpose. He chose not to do so.

Q: Well, this is going to be my last question on charge 1 then. If you turn to the transcript on 7—your Appendix 7 I believe it was. Now, can you just show the tribunal what are the precise words you rely on to suggest that Mr Galloway incited Arabs to fight British troops? Which are the actual words you rely on for that?

A: Well, they are the extracted quotes in the—

Q: Let's find them in the transcript please.

A: From recollection they occur towards the end of the interview. Let me just find them. Pretty much the final paragraph, which begins: *"Galloway: Well, let me say first of all that Iraq is fighting for all the Arabs. Why don't Arabs do something for the Iraqis?"*

Q: Let me stop you there, Mr Lennie. *"Why don't Arabs do something for the Iraqis?"* Does that say, *"Arabs must fight British troops"*?

A: It says, *"Why don't Arabs do something for the Iraqis?"*

Q: Yes. Could that only be fighting?

A: The implication—

Q: Are there no other things that that could involve?

A: The implication I take of that statement in its context following on from the first sentence that *"All Iraq is fighting for all the Arabs. Why don't Arabs do something for the Iraqis?"* and the inference I take from that is: why aren't Arabs also supporting Iraqis by fighting?

Q: Fighting. But they say—it says further down, doesn't it, *"We see Arab regimes pumping oil into the countries…[words indistinct]"*?

A: Yes. Just for completeness, sorry…

Q: Yes… [inaudible] of course were unaware of the Arab armies.

Q: Yes, we've dealt with that.

A: Arab armies—the purpose of Arab armies I guess is to fight. That's what armies do at a time of war.

Q: Where are the Arab armies you're saying he's—

A: Well—

Q: He's telling Arab armies to fight—is that what you're saying? Is that what those words mean to you?

A: It hangs in the air, yes.

Q: It hangs in the air.

A: "We wonder when the Arab leaders will wake up."

Q: You're missing out a sentence.

A: Sorry, you asked—the original question was, what are we relying on?

Q: Right.

A: And I'm just finishing for completeness the quotes extracted from the interview. And, *"When are they going to stand by the Iraqi people?"*

Q: You think the words you miss out help to explain what Mr Galloway is talking about?

> *"Even if it's not realistic to ask a non-Iraqi army to come to defend Iraq, we see Arab regimes pumping oil into the countries...* [words indistinct]. *Today 51 Iraqi civilians were killed in Baghdad by missiles fired from an Arab country...*[words indistinct]. *We wonder when the Arab leaders wake up."*

> Isn't the most reasonable interpretation of that whole paragraph that Mr Galloway was saying Arab governments ought not to be supporting the war effort? Isn't that a reasonable interpretation—whether supporting by pumping oil or firing missiles?

A: I mean—

Q: That's what Mr Galloway is saying, isn't it?

A: I don't share your interpretation. Our interpretation—my interpretation is as stated in the evidence, that the comments were intended to be heard by Arab peoples on Arab TV and inciting Arabs to fight against British troops.

Q: You use the word "intended" again. Any proof of intention?

A: They're intended to be heard by an Arab audience, that's why they're broadcast on Arab TV.

Q: But not intended to incite?

A: Inciting Arabs—the words were inciting Arabs to fight British troops. That's my interpretation of those words.

Q: Right. Your interpretation. OK.

Q: Now, charge 3 is the charge about a public meeting against the war in Plymouth, isn't it?

A: Yes. Yes, that's what it says.

Q: And the charge here is inciting again—inciting Plymouth voters to vote at the next election against Plymouth Sutton MP Linda Gilroy and Plymouth Davenport MP David Jamieson. That's your charge here.

> Now, you've been referred before to Rule 2A.4 subparagraph

(a) today, haven't you?

A: I have.

Q: Could we just turn to that for one moment please, madam. It's in the Rules. I think the page number is 2-1. Rule 2A.4(a). It's right, isn't it, under that rule that if Mr Galloway subscribed to a nomination paper, acted as an election agent—or acted as an election agent, under 2A.4(a) he would be liable for automatic expulsion? That's true, isn't it?

A: Sorry, I do apologise, I wasn't quite listening.

Q: If Mr Galloway went to Plymouth and nominated someone to stand against these MPs, Gilroy and Jamieson, or acted as their election agent, he'd obviously be liable for automatic expulsion. That's true, isn't it?

A: Yes, that's covered in the rules.

Q: Yes. And subparagraph (b), if he joined an organisation—the Liberals or somebody—who were standing in the election against Gilroy or Jamieson, or if he supported them financially, he would also be liable to automatic expulsion?

A: Yes.

Q: And of course Mr Galloway's conduct at the public meeting—the conduct you allege—doesn't fall within that rule, does it?

A: That's right.

Q: Now, do you accept that in relation to Linda Gilroy MP, the complaint she made, which you say is the only complaint you rely on, was a complaint that was first investigated by the Chief Whip of the Labour Party many months ago? Do you accept that?

A: I don't have any knowledge of that. I mean I accept that that is, you know, likely to have been the case, but I don't have any sort of detailed information from the Whip's office and so on about that.

Q: Did you interview—

A: Just let me find the—

Q: Did you interview Linda Gilroy?

A: No, I didn't interview Linda Gilroy.

Q: You didn't? You didn't interview her?

A: No, I did not.

Q: Why not?

A: Because I acted on the letter—relied upon the letter to investigate further and then received—got hold of the newspaper reports I think.

Q: Now, if you turn to that letter—it is Tab 6,

'It's nonsense for you to say—' 'It's nonsense in the English language'

page 27, 13 May—Miss Gilroy says: *"I previously made known to the Chief Whip my dissatisfaction with the behaviour of the above member."* So she states there she's previously made some kind of complaint to the Chief Whip—yes?

A: Yes.

Q: And then in the second paragraph she says: *"At the time I was satisfied that the action taken by the Chief Whip in noting my complaint was proportionate."*

A: Mmm hmm.

Q: So, she made a complaint, the Chief Whip had acted on the complaint, and she was satisfied with it. Do you accept that?

A: Yes, that's what it says. That's what it says.

Q: And then later she says:

> *"In light of the number of phone calls relating to subsequent statements by Mr Galloway in the press about the conduct of the prime minister..."*—so nothing to do with Plymouth—*"...during the conflict with Iraq I urge the NEC to seriously consider taking appropriate action."*

So she's not complaining about anything said in Plymouth, is she?

A: She's complaining about Plymouth and beyond, a continuation of what happened at Plymouth, and I think this is the nature of what our case is, that we're actually talking about—you know, this is an example of a pattern of behaviour, as we call it, in the nature of the case.

Q: So what is this pattern of behaviour?

Q: Any expression you don't like, that you think is offensive or goes too far, you say is not expression but behaviour? That's nonsense, isn't it?

A: It's nonsense for you to say—

Q: It's nonsense in the English language.

A: It's nonsense for you to say anything I don't like I describe as behaviour not expression. That is not true. What is true is that I believe these are evidences of behaviour and a pattern of behaviour exhibited by Mr Galloway, in which he seeks to attack his fellow Labour MPs in their constituencies, on websites, in order—whatever his reason is, but that is the behaviour that he undertakes.

Q: Right. Well, be that as it may, it's all very interesting again, but it's got nothing to do with charge 3, which is incitement of Plymouth voters to vote against the Plymouth MPs, and if we can just deal with that charge, because he's not charged with behaviour. Can I just ask you whether—

A: I would say incitement is a behaviour.

Q: Sorry?

A: I would say that incitement is—is a conduct.

Q: He's not charged with a pattern of behaviour, is he? He's charged with one instance of inciting in charge 3…

A: Yes.

Q: … Plymouth voters to vote against—

A: That is—

Q: So let's deal with the actual charge. Now, you rely solely for the remarks attributed to Mr Galloway on the article in the *Plymouth Gazette*, which is at Appendix 12, page 41. Is that right?

A: That's right.

Q: That's the only evidence you've got of what Mr Galloway said at that meeting?

A: Provided in evidence.

Q: Do you know if the *Plymouth Gazette* is a Labour paper?

A: I haven't sought to enquire. What I do know is that there is no attempt to correct the account of the meeting that took place and was reported by the Plymouth newspaper.

Q: So you hadn't sought to enquire from the journalist, for instance, Matt Fleming, exactly what was said. Is that right?

A: Well, I've relied upon the quotes.

Q: Relied upon the quotes. Have you asked anybody in the Plymouth Labour Party what was said?

A: I haven't asked anyone in the Plymouth Labour Party what was said, I've relied upon the quotes. That's why they're there.

Q: And your investigation was so perfunctory that you preferred the words in a local paper and you didn't investigate further. You didn't ask for notes of the meeting, you didn't contact anybody there, you didn't ask Mr Galloway what he said. You just took the word of the paper and said, "Right, you're inciting people to vote against MPs." That's how thorough your investigation was.

A: Well, I'm relying on the quotes from Mr Galloway's own mouth, yes.

Q: Well, come on, Mr Lennie, you can't keep trying to pull the wool over the eyes of this panel. You're relying on the quotes attributed to him by a journalist in a local paper.

A: I'm relying on the quotes in the paper attributed to Mr Galloway. As I've said before, for the fourth time, uncorrected. There isn't any attempt to seek correction if they are wrong, therefore in terms of evidence they're reliable.

Q: Have you any idea how many local public meetings Mr Galloway attends in the course of the year?

A: I don't know that.

Q: Did you expect that he reads, checks and corrects what's reported about him in every local newspaper when he has to contend with papers like the *Daily Telegraph* publishing libels of him? Is that really what you expect Mr Galloway to spend his time doing?

A: I would expect it is the practice of all Labour MPs if they are quoted wrongly—and that is a serious matter in terms of what they're quoted as having said or incited—to correct the record, yes.

Q: Let me just ask you a question. You said that this was a taped meeting and that you'd been supplied a tape. I understand you said a female student, is that right?

A: That's all I know, yes, a female student I understand from Lancaster University.

Q: And did you pay this student to tape the meeting?

A: I don't know who she was.

Q: How did you receive the tape?

A: It was sent to the Labour Party. I don't even know when it came into the Labour Party. It was then passed to me subsequently. Well, in fact it was passed and it was translated into the transcription by our media monitoring unit and then the transcription was passed to me.

Q: Well, as part of the investigation then did you look into the circumstances in which this meeting was tape recorded?

A: I didn't regard them as relevant.

Q: You didn't regard them as relevant?

A: No. I wanted to establish the fact as to whether this was a reliable transcription of that meeting—a tape recording and subsequent transcription of the meeting, and I believe it is a reliable piece of evidence of what happened at that meeting.

Q: Is it usual for you to receive tape cassettes secretly taped of public meetings sent to you in order to bolster up complaints against MPs you don't like? Is that a usual occurrence?

A: Well, this is a unique circumstance for me so therefore it isn't a usual occurrence. This has not happened before. I have not been involved in investigating this case or a case comparable before and, therefore, it hasn't arisen, so it could not be a usual circumstance.

Q: Now, this is perhaps a far less unfortunately hypothetical situation,

Mr Lennie. Consider for a moment that in the North of England somewhere there had been a by-election, perhaps a council by-election, and the Liberal Democrat beat a sitting BNP councillor, and Labour stood in that election as it always did but all the parties were concerned to beat a racist BNP councillor. After the election a Labour MP came to the constituency and said"Let me say how proud I am that…" whoever it is "…elected an anti-racist Liberal Democrat candidate who's also a Welshman." Would that to you be something that you would be interested in bringing disciplinary charges about?

'Did you pay this student to tape the meeting?'

A: Can I repeat pretty much what I said before. The situation hasn't arisen where I've been asked to investigate those circumstances. I'd need to look at all the circumstances that applied should such a reference be made and investigated and, as the chair has said, subject to whatever that investigation produced, and so on and so forth. Can I just say generally, in relation to the co-ordination and the mechanics between parties in opposition and in united opposition to other parties, there are situations that could arise, and probably have arisen, where parties have even agreed to liken the campaign or co-ordinate together against a united extreme force of one sort or another. I can envisage that circumstance. I can envisage the management of that circumstance. That is not the circumstance that we're dealing with in Preston. The most obvious example of that kind of circumstance was probably Tatton.

Q: Well, if there was no such agreement everybody was up for the seat but the Liberals won. Is it really bringing the into prejudice to say, "I'm proud that Burnley elected an anti-racist Liberal candidate." Of course it's not, is it?

A: Well, I think the hypotheticals—and in relation to what constitutes the subject of the investigation and potential to that investigation leading to an NCC panel hearing, I don't have anything to draw upon because the circumstance hasn't arisen and I've not been asked to investigate it.

Q: Would it be your case that such a comment would be prejudicial?

A: Again I repeat what I said before. If the circumstance arises and I'm asked to investigate it I will do so and draw a conclusion. I'm not prepared to speculate upon the hypothesis that might arise without knowing what the circumstances in total are before I reach conclusions. I

Charge Five

understand your anxiety or your concern to draw me to a conclusion but you're not going to get there so, with respect, I think it's a fairly fruitless scrutiny.

Q: Mr Lennie, the truth is that you'd never be asked to investigate such a thing because it would be ludicrous and a waste of time to investigate such a thing, so the situation would never arise?

A: I've said the situation hasn't arisen. It's not my experience, I've not been asked to do it. If and when it does arise and I am, then we'll have something to go on but, as things stand, it hasn't arisen.

Q: But the only difference here, the only difference here, is that Mr Galloway is congratulating an anti-war Socialist and not an anti-racist Liberal and that you're trying to expel Mr Galloway from the party. That's the only difference, isn't it?

A: The situation, as I said before, has arisen in the past where we've had co-ordination between otherwise opposition parties in order to defeat a common opposing candidate. The most obvious one, and I'll quote it again, is Tatton when Martin Bell was elected as an independent against the sitting Conservative in the light of the "cash for questions" scandal, Neil Hamilton. So the situation of co-ordinated political management between otherwise opposition parties can arise. It was not the case where there was that situation in Preston in the May elections of 2003.

Q: Now, I'll suggest to you, Mr Lennie, that if Mr Galloway had made these comments before the election, comments along the lines of "Preston should elect an anti-war socialist candidate" you would be right in bringing these charges. I don't think we're in dispute about that, is that right?

A: My charges are that the expression of Mr Galloway, the expression of his pride—the expression of pride is beyond an opinion and belief but is an action for support for the outcome of that election made on the success of the Socialist Alliance candidate against the official candidate. That is my contention and that is the charge that we have brought.

Q: Are you not at all concerned at the damage you're doing to the English language in this hearing?—

The chair: Is that relevant?

Mr De Marco: Is that relevant? It's entirely relevant.

The chair: We're not here to judge the English language, Mr De Marco.

Mr De Marco: Well, it's ordinary meanings of words, madam—

The chair: I know where you're coming from.

Mr De Marco: ...and we've had the general secretary of the Labour

Party suggest that expressing pride cannot be expression. It's a remarkable thing to listen to.

A: Beyond mere expression is what I've said. Can I just say I have read the overnight reports that quote me, I think from Mr Galloway or his supporters, as either distorting or inventing in mendacious, pitiful and demeaning language—

Mr Galloway: And degrading.

A: ...and degrading. So I'm aware of the way in which my evidence has been received by you, or by Mr Galloway, but it is my intention to—

Mr Galloway: Luckily we have a transcript.

A: ...to re-establish encyclopaedic English.

Mr De Marco: In any event, Mr Lennie, there's no dispute, is there, that these comments were made six weeks after an election?

A: There's no dispute about when they were made—6 June 2003.

Q: And there therefore was no prejudice to the Labour Party?

A: There was prejudice to the Labour Party. There is continuing prejudice to the Labour Party. The comments were made, the expression of pride on the outcome of that election.

Q: What is the prejudice?

A: The prejudice is the demonstrable support by Mr Galloway for a candidate who was the opposition candidate to the official Labour candidate.

Q: Again, just to get our facts right, not to a candidate but to someone who was no longer a candidate, that's the prejudice?

A: The successful candidate. Yes, you're right, the then councillor.

Q: That's the prejudice?

A: Yes.

George Galloway cross-examined by Nicholas De Marco

Q: I just would like to ask very briefly the following five questions and then I will have no further questions. The first is that, in relation to charge 1, did you ever incite Arabs to fight British troops?

A: No.

Q: Secondly, in relation to charge 2, did you ever incite British troops to disobey orders?

A: Only illegal orders.

Q: Thirdly, in relation to charge 3, did you incite Plymouth voters to vote at the next general election against Plymouth Sutton Labour MP, Linda Gilroy, and Plymouth Devonport Labour MP, David Jamieson?

A: I have spent virtually my entire life inciting people to vote Labour. I have never ever anywhere incited anyone to vote against Labour.

Q: Fourthly, Did you threaten to fight the Glasgow Central constituency in certain circumstances as an independent, that is against a duly endorsed Labour candidate?

A: No.

Q: And finally did you at a public meeting in Preston support one Michael Lavalette, having stood in local elections in May 2003 against the duly endorsed Labour candidate, Musa Ahmed Jiwa?

A: Only someone practising the Orwellian distortion of the English language could interpret my comments in Preston, secretly tape recorded, as giving support to a candidate which stood against the Labour Party.

George Galloway cross-examined by James Goudie QC

Q: Is there anything at all that you apologise for?

A: In my life?

Q: No, in relation to the subject matter of these proceedings?

A: Certainly not.

Q: Is there anything that you do not stand by so far as what you have said relating to these proceedings?

A: No.

Q: Could you take the NEC bundle, please, and turn to Appendix 8 which is page 31 to 33, being the ITV News Channel on 1 April this year?

A: Yes.

Q: Do you stand by everything you said on that occasion or is there anything you're prepared to apologise for?

A: Well, I would wish to put in context that which is not in the transcript but which immediately preceded it, which was a brutish attack upon me by the armed forces minister, Adam Ingram. I make that point because I wouldn't want the panel to think that I willy-nilly embarked upon an ad hominem attack on Adam Ingram for no reason. I would want you to know that immediately prior to the beginning of this transcript a very personal and vicious attack on me had been launched by Mr Ingram. Other than that I stand by every word that I said.

Q: And at this paragraph:

"Let's go to the heart of the issue. I did not call the British armed forces 'wolves', indeed I called them 'lions'. I did not call upon the British armed forces to disobey orders, I called upon them to disobey illegal orders. As you well know this is in fact a legal obligation on them, as on all armies and on all governments since Nuremberg..."

My specific question is this—do you stand by your use of the language "called upon"?

A: Yes, and the fact is that I assumed that the general secretary is aware that it is a legal obligation. Unfortunately his deputy was not so aware, but the general secretary must be aware that it is an obligation on all armies since Nuremberg to disobey illegal orders, and of course I called upon the British army to disobey illegal orders, as I call upon all armies everywhere to disobey illegal orders.

Q: Thank you. Then the penultimate paragraph of the letter:

"I've never threatened to stand as an independent if I 'am not selected' in Glasgow. I've made the same statement over and over again which is this. If the local members of the new Glasgow Central constituency are freely allowed to choose their candidate, I will of course respect their decision. If, however, the members are robbed of a free selection by an administrative method or trumped up disciplinary charges, then that would be a different matter. In those circumstances, which I'm sure you would not contemplate, I would of course have to consider my position."

Do you stand by that?

A: I do indeed.

Q: And at Appendix 13 at page 45—well Appendix 13, this is the Newsnight interview, begins at page 42 but we get at the last question and answer on page 45. Mr Paxman I think said:

"Just to be clear on this question of your involvement with the Labour Party, your seat is going to be abolished. Will you seek re-nomination to Labour candidacy at the next election?" Answer: *"Well, my seat isn't going to be abolished. Glasgow's going to be three seats and the remaining seven are merging, so mine is no more being abolished than anyone else's. But of course I shall seek for nomination in the Glasgow Central constituency. If the members are allowed to do so I think I can confidently predict that they will select me. If they are cheated of that right then of course I will defend the seat as an independent."*

Do you stand by that?

A: I do.

Q: And who will be the judge of whether they are robbed or cheated?

A: Well, like the camel, that will be difficult to define hypothetically but easy to recognise. If I am precluded by administrative methods or trumped up disciplinary charges from placing myself before the members of the

'Even he is finding it difficult to press these trumped-up charges'

Glasgow Central Constituency Labour Party for selection, then the members will have, ipso facto, have been robbed, cheated, of the opportunity to select me.

Q: How are they cheated or robbed, by what you regard as trumped up charges, unless the NCC regard them as well founded charges?

A: Well, anyone reading these proceedings—and I thank god that they will read these proceedings—will—can only conclude that Mr Lennie's investigation and his indictment is a trumped up charge by any reasonable person's definition. Anyone who has witnessed the tortuous—tortuous perversions of the English language in which he has been involved over hour after hour in these proceedings can only conclude that even he is finding it difficult to press these trumped-up charges without embarrassment.

Q: And having begun that paragraph by the reference to "fighting" and then concluding it: "We wonder when the Arab leaders wake up whether they're going to stand by the Iraqi people." Doesn't that obviously mean standing by the Iraqi people, including by way of fighting alongside them, supporting them in their fight?

A: Only if you're prosecuting a trumped-up charge. That's the only way in which you could possibly interpret these words as meaning that. I have not hypothetically, as you just have, but actually in the same paragraph given two examples of ways in which the Arab regimes could stand by the Iraqi people—by stopping pumping oil to the people attacking them and stopping allowing their territory to be used for that attack. "Why look in the crystal ball when you can read the book?" as Nye Bevan once said.

Nicholas De Marco's closing statement

Mr Galloway has established in this case that this case is about one thing and one thing only. The Presenter doesn't want to refer to this and certainly doesn't want to acknowledge it but Mr Galloway is the most outspoken Member of Parliament to oppose the most unpopular war this country has ever been involved in. Mr Galloway was one of the most prominent leaders of the anti-war movement. He is known to have strong, genuinely held, passionate beliefs about justice for Palestinians and about the wrongs of this Iraq war and the years of sanctions that were levied against Iraq.

Mr Galloway has never once sought to hide any of his views and it's because of his strong views and his prominent position in the anti-war movement that he became the bogeyman of the right wing press, in particular the *Sun* and the *Daily Telegraph*, during the most unpopular war this country has ever been involved in. The *Sun* newspaper, assisted by Labour armed forces minister, Adam Ingram, labelled Mr Galloway a "Traitor" across the front page of their edition and encouraged readers to "phone up and harass him and suggested he be tried for treason and sent to prison for life". The *Sun* encouraged the very hate mail that was not only sent to Mr Galloway but you saw some of in the folder produced by the NEC Presenter as complaints they say they had received—the type of mail that said, for instance, "Isn't it disgraceful Tony Martin is languishing in jail when a traitor like Galloway is out on the streets." That kind of disgusting hate mail, the kind of hate mail which said, "Mr Galloway sucks Saddam's toes and he can come and suck mine in Belfast if I put a moustache on." This kind of ludicrous nonsense that in fact you may wish to bear some consideration, madam, were those two complaints I referred to, were amongst those the NEC Presenter said they relied on and were not amongst those they said were offensive and ones they didn't rely on.

The *Daily Telegraph* went even further than the *Sun* and produced the ultimate slur against Mr Galloway—they said he was in the pay of Saddam Hussein. They said that he was paid in oil money to oppose the war. Looking back, madam, any reasonable person can see how ludicrous these slurs were.

You may or may not be familiar with the Zinoviev letter, but it was on a par with that episode, when a letter was fabricated by enemies of the Labour Party to discredit a Labour Party in an election and suggest that the enemy supported the Labour leadership—and the thought that a lone journalist picking over the wrecks of the Iraqi information ministry could find a document showing that Mr Galloway was in Iraq's pay, when weapons of mass destruction still cannot be found and when all the coalition forces in Iraq cannot find the most wanted man in the world, Saddam Hussein, that thought would be laughable if it was not for the pain and damage it did for an honest MP who stood up for his beliefs, and the insult to the integrity that slur cast on all those who opposed the most disastrous war this country has been involved in for many, many years.

Madam, that is the background to these charges. It doesn't matter how much the NEC Presenter or Mr Goudie protest otherwise, it doesn't matter how much one tries to recoil from that fact, everybody outside knows that that's what these charges are about and everybody outside knows that if Mr Galloway is expelled it's because he was the most outspoken critic of the war.

It's against this background, of a fantastic and hysterical campaign against Mr Galloway, that the Labour general secretary, prompted by an interview in the *Sun* attributed to Mr Blair, within days of these stories, suspended Mr Galloway, we say in breach of the party's rules, and the NEC Presenter has been unable to show otherwise, but it was in response to this campaign, this hysterical campaign against Mr Galloway that this action was taken.

Then Mr Lennie comes on the scene, and I'm not sure if he's still here but he then came on the scene and it was his job to cook up these charges. Madam, you've looked at the charges and you've heard the evidence and it's impossible, I would say, having heard the evidence and looked at the charges, to find any other than that these charges were manufactured, they're badly drawn up, they don't relate properly to the rules and I will deal with each one individually in turn. But, madam, the decision was taken. Mr Lennie probably didn't make it but was probably told, "Get Galloway, get him out of the party, manufacture the charges, produce what evidence you can get hold of..."—and it's the most unreliable one could imagine—"...and the NCC will rubber stamp it." That's probably what he was told about the NCC. I don't believe that—

Mr Goudie: This is outrageous. I mean—

Mr De Marco: Mr Goudie, please, I didn't interrupt you, please—

Tony Woodley, general secretary of the Transport and General Workers Union

I consider the current proceedings against George Galloway to be unacceptable and completely unjustified. I consider that George Galloway is subject to a witch-hunt brought about because of his opposition to the war. I believe that had George Galloway not been so vociferous in his opposition to the war he would not face many of the actions that he does today and he certainly would not face an action to expel him from the Labour Party.

Mr Goudie: No, and you had no cause to.

Mr De Marco: If you want to respond to what I have to say you can at the end of my—

The chair: Mr De Marco, please. Gentlemen, could we please not have this sort of crossfire.

Mr Goudie: That last remark that was made by Mr De Marco was absolutely and utterly disgraceful and he should withdraw it. That's all I wish to say.

Mr De Marco: Madam, I can't withdraw that remark because that remark has been repeated in the press on many occasions. It's not one I associate myself with and I was saying that when Mr Goudie was interrupting me. What I am saying—what I am submitting and what Mr Galloway believes is that these charges were fabricated from the beginning with the intention to expel Mr Galloway and Mr Lennie believed that this would be an operation that would not be particularly difficult. I believe and hope he is wrong in that.

Madam, I suggest a reason why that's the case is that when this action was originally taken against Mr Galloway those responsible for it, including I suppose Mr Lennie, thought that Mr Galloway's political career was over. They believed that the war in Iraq had been a great success or was about to be a great success and they believed, or thought others would, the absurd story in the *Daily Telegraph*. They believed that expelling Mr Galloway would be an uncontroversial and perhaps even a popular act. They may have reasonably believed that at the time, madam, but six months on it's you, the panel of the NCC, who is faced with a completely different set of circumstances and a much more difficult decision from that standpoint than existed six months ago, because—and the reason for this is simple—six months on the war in Iraq, which is the background to every one of these charges, is in reality still going on. More coalition forces have been killed in fighting since the formal end of hostilities than during them. The Iraqi resistance to the occupation has grown. Terrorism and fundamentalism has spread across the whole region. The much-trumpeted Middle East road map has crashed amongst the wreckage of suicide bombs and Israeli attacks in Syria. No weapons of mass destruction have been found, the search for them has all but finished. Indeed, many from Robin Cook—and this is in the bundle—to Hans Blix say that Iraq never had these